epic adventure

Epic Climbs

EIGER ▲ K2 ▲ EVEREST ▲ McKINLEY ▲ MATTERHORN

KINGFISHER
LONDON & NEW YORK

Published in the United States by Kingfisher,
175 Fifth Ave., New York, NY 10010
Kingfisher is an imprint of Macmillan Children's Books, London.
All rights reserved

Distributed in the U.S. by Macmillan,
175 Fifth Ave., New York, NY 10010
Distributed in Canada by H.B. Fenn and Company Ltd.,
34 Nixon Road, Bolton, Ontario L7E 1W2

Conceived and produced by Weldon Owen Pty Ltd
59–61 Victoria Street, McMahons Point
Sydney, NSW 2060, Australia
Copyright © 2010 Weldon Owen Pty Ltd
First printed 2010

WELDON OWEN PTY LTD

Chief Executive Officer Sheena Coupe
Publisher Corinne Roberts
Creative Director Sue Burk

Senior Vice President, International Sales Stuart Laurence
Sales Manager: United States Ellen Towell
Vice President, Sales: Asia and Latin America Dawn L. Owen
Administration Manager, International Sales Kristine Ravn
Production Manager Todd Rechner
Production Coordinators Lisa Conway, Mike Crowton
Production Assistant Nathan Grice

Concept Design Arthur Brown/Cooling Brown
Senior Editor Averil Moffat
Designer John Bull/The Book Design Company
Cartography Will Pringle, Mapgraphx
Art Manager Trucie Henderson
Picture Research Joanna Collard
Editorial Assistant Natalie Ryan

Index Jo Rudd

Library of Congress Cataloging-in-Publication data has been applied for.

ISBN: 978-0-7534-6573-8

Kingfisher books are available for special promotions and premiums.
For details contact: Special Markets Department, Macmillan,
175 Fifth Avenue, New York, NY 10010

For more information, please visit www.kingfisherbooks.com

Printed by Toppan Leefung Printing Limited

Manufactured in China
10 9 8 7 6 5 4 3 2 1

The paper used in the manufacture of this book is sourced from
wood grown in sustainable forests. It complies with the
Environmental Management System Standard ISO 14001:2004

A WELDON OWEN PRODUCTION

epic adventure

Epic Climbs

EIGER ▲ K2 ▲ EVEREST ▲ McKINLEY ▲ MATTERHORN →

John Cleare

KINGFISHER
NEW YORK

introduction

What is the secret drive that inspires people to climb to the summit of high mountains? Mountaineers themselves would have many different answers. For some it is the technical challenge of the climb, every small movement requiring careful judgment. And there is a physical challenge, the need to conserve and focus energy to last the distance. There is also the pleasure to be found in exercising familiar skills and climbing safely among the astonishing rock architecture of mountain landscapes. Survival at high altitudes is a mental challenge, too. Thin air slows reactions and makes decision-making difficult, so climbers must draw on every resource to remain alert and aware. No wonder, then, that reaching a hard-won summit is such an exciting and memorable experience.

contents

THE Eiger

The Ogre in the Alps

Three great peaks form the northern edge of the Bernese Alps, an abrupt wall looking out across the Swiss lowlands to the plains of northern Europe. Highest is the beautiful, snowy Jungfrau (The Maiden), next is the Mönch (The Monk). On the left is the imposing Eiger (The Ogre), the name well describing its intimidating appearance. Unlike many other alpine peaks, this so-called "Bernese Oberland" is easily approached; small towns and villages dot the foothills. The Jungfrau was first climbed as long ago as 1813, from its southern side above the extensive glaciers of the Aletsch system, more than 38 square miles (100 km²) of continuous ice. Here nearly 50 peaks of 12,000 feet (3,655 m) or more make a playground for alpinists and ski-mountaineers.

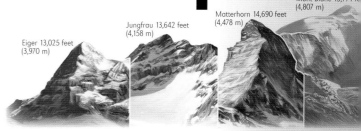

Eiger 13,025 feet (3,970 m)

Jungfrau 13,642 feet (4,158 m)

Matterhorn 14,690 feet (4,478 m)

Mont Blanc 15,771 feet (4,807 m)

Four Peaks
L-R: Eiger, a pyramid of rock and ice; Jungfrau, snow ridges and glaciers; Matterhorn, a rock spire; Mont Blanc, a huge white dome.

Bernese Alps
The Bernese Alps, part of the Western Alps, stretch some 70 miles (112 km) east from Lake Geneva. The Eiger stands near the north-eastern extremity.

Andreas Hinterstoisser fell to his death; of the three others on the rope two were also dead.

Kurz cut Willy Angerer's body free, hoping to gain more rope. But it was still too short to save him.

Toni Kurz

Toni Kurz and Andreas Hinterstoisser teamed up with Edi Rainer and Willy Angerer to attempt the North Face in 1936. Reaching a blank wall, Hinterstoisser discovered how to traverse it with ropes, which the climbers removed once they were across. Angerer was injured by falling stones and they began to retreat. But they were unable to recross the Hinterstoisser Traverse, so had to abseil down a 655-foot (200-m) wall. On their fourth day a storm hit.

FATAL FALL
In the storm, Hinterstoisser fell and Angerer and Rainer, probably hit by stones, died of exposure tangled in the ropes. The remaining rope was not quite long enough for Kurz to reach the rescuers below. Despite his efforts to climb down, he died there (right).

Inside the Mountain

In 1897 work began on boring a tunnel four and a half miles (7 km) through the heart of the Eiger and the Monch. It linked Kleine Scheidegg by electric rack railway to the ice-hung saddle of the Jungfraujoch, 4,575 feet (1,395 m) higher. Here an observatory was built and tourist facilities constructed in a large gallery. Occasional side tunnels, "Stollenloch", were cut so that rubble could be tipped out. The railway, the Jungfraubahn, was completed in 1912.

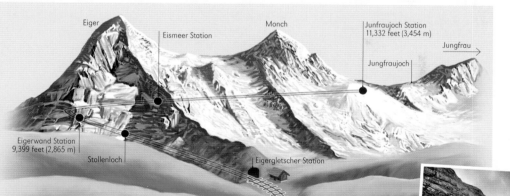

Eiger

Eismeer Station

Monch

Junfraujoch Station
11,332 feet (3,454 m)

Jungfrau →

Jungfraujoch

Eigerwand Station
9,399 feet (2,865 m)

Stollenloch

Eigergletscher Station

← To Kleine Scheidegg

Electric locomotive in use c 1925.

There are two intermediate stations, galleries carved into the living rock, where trains pass and passengers alight for a few minutes to admire the view from large windows set into the face of the mountain.

Climbers and ski-mountaineers can walk out of the gallery at Eismeer and step onto the glacier.

Before windows were fitted, visitors could enjoy the view from a platform where the gallery opened onto the mountain's face.

Success on the North Face

Discovering a feasible, relatively safe route up the Eigerwand was a formidable problem. Max Sedlmayer and Karl Mehringer, the first to try, spent days studying the face through binoculars. The steep limestone often runs with meltwater and the hanging ice fields are iron-hard and frequently swept by falling stones. In bad weather, powder avalanches pour down the face. Safe bivouac sites are few. Hard overnight frost and settled weather are prerequisites for safety. Despite courage and their prowess on the steep limestone of the Eastern Alps, none of the Eigerwand pioneers had previously encountered climbs of this scale. Also, because the Eigerwand rises sheer from the meadows, climbers are in the public eye—their every move can be followed by tourists and the press through a battery of telescopes at Kleine Scheidegg in the valley below.

Danger From Above
Rockfall is a major hazard. The continuous cycle of freezing and thawing cracks and splinters the rock. Then sun or warm weather melts the ice and pieces of rock fall. Avalanches of new powder snow, and other climbers above, may also dislodge stones.

KEY ACHIEVEMENTS ON THE EIGER			
1938	Heinrich Harrer Fritz Kasparek	Andreas Heckmair Ludwig Vorg	First successful ascent
1961	Toni Kinshofer Toni Hiebeler	Anderl Mannhardt Walter Almberger	First winter ascent
1963	Michel Darbellay		First solo ascent
1973	Wanda Rutkiewicz	Danuta Wach Stefania Egierszdorff	First all-female rope
2008	Ueli Steck		Fastest solo ascent ever

Four at the Summit

In 1938, two experienced German climbers caught up with two capable young Austrians below the Death Bivouac and joined forces to make a powerful team. Despite several falls, minor injuries, a fierce storm, snow-plastered rock, and finding a route up virgin terrain, they reached the summit after three bivouacs. They descended safely via the West Flank.

Newsworthy

The four climbers were feted throughout alpine countries and their achievement was described in *The Illustrated London News* (right). Many had thought the North Face would never be climbed.

FOUR MEN OUTWIT THE OGRE MOUNTAIN: THE "UNSCALEABLE" EIGER NORTH FACE CLIMBED.

THE ILLUSTRATED LONDON NEWS

HERR HECKMEIR, OF MUNICH.   HERR VÖRG, OF MUNICH.   HERR KASPAREK, OF VIENNA.   HERR HARRER, OF VIENNA.

THE FOUR WHO CLIMBED THE "UNSCALEABLE" EIGER NORTH FACE.

The Climbers

The successful climbers after their safe descent, left to right: Heinrich Harrer, Ludwig Vorg, Andreas Heckmair, and Fritz Kasparek. Heckmair and Vorg, both from Munich, were experienced climbers. Kasparek and Harrer, both from Vienna, were younger but had fine climbing records.

Overnight Rest

Bivouacs were made on a suitable ledge, safely roped under a tent sack. The climbers brewed hot drinks from snow-melt on a tiny spirit-cooker.

Helicopters have revolutionized alpine rescue; few places are out of reach of a rescuer swinging below a helicopter.

Special stretchers are used for mountain casualties but they are awkward and heavy to maneuver.

Rescues

Mountaineers are honor-bound to assist their fellows in distress, but rescue on the Eigerwand was long considered impossible. In 1957 two Italian climbers, Claudio Corti and Stefano Longhi, were approaching the White Spider when Longhi was injured in a fall. Leaving him hanging on the rope, Corti continued to the Spider where, injured himself, he bivouacked. But the accident had been noticed, climbers mobilized from all over the Alps, and the latest rescue gear was manhandled to the summit. Alfred Hellepart was lowered 1,000 feet (300 m) on a thin steel cable to piggyback Corti, after nine days on the North Face, to safety. A storm broke before Longhi could be reached and his body remained hanging there for two years.

Amazing Feat

The Corti rescue amazed the alpine world. The Grindelwald Chief Guide believed that rescue was impossible, but many others disagreed. The Munich Rescue Team had the equipment, and alpinists were determined to help one of their fellows. Only a massive effort, and Hellepart's courage, saved Corti's life.

After the Pioneers

Once it was known to be possible, the North Face climb was first repeated in 1947 by the great French guides Lionel Terray and Louis Lachenal, and by 13 further parties in the following decade. Tragedies still occurred but more and more of the best alpinists succeeded on the North Face and new challenges were accepted—a winter ascent, solo, and first female ascents, and then a direct ascent straight up the center. By the 1980s the Eigerwand had become the goal of ambitious alpinists of every nation and the most intrepid were forging new routes. Global warming and shrinking ice fields have increased the dangers but there are now some 30 different lines. Winter has become the favorite season for climbers to try the North Face. The weather is more stable and modern clothing and equipment suit the conditions.

SPEED CLIMB
The fastest ascent so far, though not his first, was made by Swiss guide Ueli Steck, solo, in 2 hours 47 minutes in February 2008.

Climbing Boots

The 1938 alpine boots were leather and nailed but three of the successful party also used crampons. Crampons are essential with Vibram soles. Modern climbers wear insulated double-boots.

Nailed sole   Vibram sole

Nails and Cleats
Climbing boot soles were nailed until the cleated rubber Vibram sole—invented by Vitale Bramani in 1935—came into general use in the 1950s.

Experienced climbers had their own favorite nails and nailing patterns. (1) the hard steel Tricouni (2) the soft iron Clinker (3) the Star Mugger.

CHAMPION CLIMBER
Wanda Rutkiewicz, from Poland, led the first all-female team up the Eigerwand in 1973, making the second ascent of the new North Pillar route. An experienced high altitude mountaineer and the leading female climber of her day, she disappeared attempting a solo climb in 1992 on Kangchenjunga in the East Nepal Himalaya.

List of Route Names

1. Lauper Route
2. Scottish North East Pillar
3. Slovenian Route
4. Harlin Direct Route
5. Metanoia
6. Japanese Direct
7. 1938 Route
8. Ghillini-Piola Direct
9. The Swan-song
10. Ochsner-Brunner Route

MULTIPLE ROUTES

As climbers sought fresh challenges, more new routes on the North Face were tried for the first time. Each route involves many difficult sections and reaching the summit is an achievement for even the most experienced climber.

Eastwood, no climber, bravely insisted on performing his own stunts. Here he prepares for a "fall" scene with some 3,000 feet (1,000 m) of space beneath his feet

In a sequence based on the Toni Kurtz tragedy—although not this time in a fierce storm—Clint Eastwood dangles over the Stollenloch gallery window.

This lightweight tripod could be rigged almost anywhere to dangle climbers or camermen.

Filming the *Eiger Sanction*

In 1974 the actor and director Clint Eastwood made the bold decision to film the novel *Eiger Sanction*, a spy thriller set on and around the Eiger's North Face. A strong team of British and American climbers and mountain cameramen joined the actors at Kleine Scheidegg and spent six weeks shooting some spectacular film, although the most dangerous areas of the North Face were avoided.

Clint Eastwood

K2

The Karakoram

The Karakoram Range stands north of the Himalaya where India, Pakistan, and China meet. Four of the world's fourteen peaks that exceed 26,000 feet (8,000 m) rise here amid a vast area of magnificent ice-hung mountains, savage rock pillars, immense glaciers, and steep gorges. It is inhospitable, arid country sparsely inhabited by Balti and Hunza tribespeople whose meager villages, surrounded by fields and orchards, cling to ledges in the deep valleys. For a long time this region was inaccessible and politically sensitive. In the 19th century it was of interest to Czarist Russia to its north and British India to its south. The first exploration and mapping of the Karakoram was the result of competition between the two empires. They both wanted to know more about the remote region that lay between them. It is still a sensitive region today; the Indo–Pakistan Kashmir Ceasefire Line cuts across the southeastern corner of the range.

ADVENTURER
Sir Francis Younghusband (1863–1942) has been called the Last Great Imperial Adventurer. As a cavalry officer in India, a mountain explorer, and later as a soldier-diplomat and mystic, he traveled widely in the Karakoram, one of few Englishmen to do so.

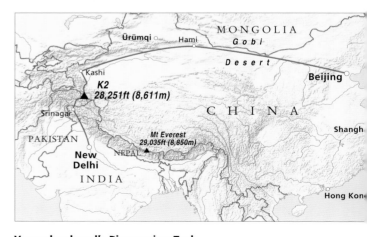

Younghusband's Pioneering Trek
In 1887, returning to India from Peking (now Beijing), Younghusband rode across the Gobi Desert and through the unexplored Kun Lun and Aghil ranges. He passed K2 on its northern side and crossed into India via the Muztagh Pass.

NORTHERN FLANK

The distant "Karakoram Peak 2" was seen by a British surveyor in 1856 and first approached in 1861 by Col. Godwin Austen when he was mapping the Baltoro Glacier. He confirmed the height of K2.

Apart from sightings by Younghusband and Czarist Capt. Grombezewski in the 1880s, the imposing Chinese (northern) flank of K2 was unknown until it was explored in the 1930s.

Military Mission

In 1903–04 Younghusband led a military mission to remote Lhasa. His intention was to demand a treaty of co-operation with Britain. This plan, which would have given Britain some influence in the region, was not without opposition. In the illustration above, troops of the Indian Army storm a hilltop fort.

ARID LANDSCAPE

In 1892 Martin Conway, an art historian and keen alpinist, led a climbing and exploring expedition, supported by the Royal Geographical Society, into the arid Braldu Valley (right) to explore the Baltoro Glacier in detail. He named Concordia, Broad Peak, and Hidden Peak (Gasherbrum I), reached the foot of K2, and climbed the 22,598-foot (6,888m) Pioneer Peak.

FIRST PHOTOGRAPHS

The Duke of Abruzzi's 1909 expedition closely examined the south, east, and west flanks of K2. Among the group was Vittorio Sella (1859–1943), regarded as the best of early mountain photographers. He also climbed and photographed in the Himalaya, the Caucasus, Africa, and Alaska. This is his photograph of K2's west flank above the Savoia Glacier.

Trekking to K2

Any approach to K2 is an expedition in its own right. On the usual, southern, route from Pakistan everything must be carried by local porters. A four-wheel-drive track, frequently cut by landslides, now follows the hazardous Braldu Gorge to Askole, the last habitation. Previously this stretch took four strenuous days on foot. Continuing up the valley and crossing the tributary Dumorda River, it takes three days of hard trekking to reach the snout of the Baltoro Glacier. After four more days this avenue of endless moraines, with few decent camp sites but lined with spectacular peaks, leads to Concordia, the wide glacial T-junction from where K2 is at last visible. From here the mountain is a mere day's march northward up the Godwin Austen Glacier. This is the easy way—approach to the northern side of K2, from barren Xinjiang, is even more demanding.

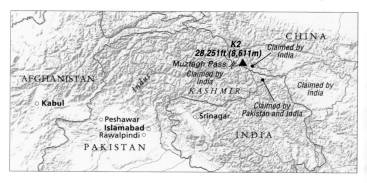

BALTI PORTERS
Expedition porters enjoy an impromptu dance on reaching an overnight camp en route to K2. Strict regulations govern their pay, loads, and stage lengths. Baltis are fiercely proud and often belligerent; arguments about their work conditions occasionally occur.

Locating K2
K2 stands on the Pakistan-Chinese border in a forest of savage peaks, surrounded by huge glaciers that drain south to the Indus River or north to high Asian deserts.

The First Ascent

The Duke of Abruzzi's 1909 expedition had given Italian climbers a special interest in K2 and in July 1954, Professor Ardito Desio mounted a large, nationally backed expedition of 11 climbers, four scientists, a doctor, and a filmmaker. They planned to use oxygen—not used previously on K2. Each oxygen set weighed 40 pounds (18 kg) and consequently some 700 porters were employed for the march-in. After two weeks' climbing, Camp 4 was pitched below House's Chimney. But the weather was poor, Mario Puchoz died from pulmonary edema, and morale sagged. Desio, himself a non-climber, sent a message to the lead team telling them that the honor of Italian mountaineering was at stake. But six weeks passed before Compagnoni and Lacedelli established Camp 8 at 25,400 feet (7,740 m) just below the Shoulder. They were supported by Bonatti, the youngest but most talented climber, and Gallotti. All were exhausted.

EXPEDITIONERS
The 1954 expedition at Base Camp. Back (l–r): Achille Compagnoni, Ugo Angelino, Dr. Gino Pagani, Mario Fantin, Ardito Desio, Erich Abram, Gino Soldà, Lino Lacedelli, Walter Bonatti, Sergio Viotto, Pino Gallotti. Front: Ubaldo Rey, Cirillo Floreanini, and Mario Puchoz.

SOUTHERN FLANK
The great southern flank of K2 rears some 11,500 feet (3,500 m) over the Godwin Austen Glacier.

Three Attempts

Duke of Abruzzi

Martin Conway's expedition first reached the foot of K2 in 1892 and 10 years later Oscar Eckenstein's team set foot on the Northeast Ridge. But after the Duke of Abruzzi's 1909 expedition had identified the "Abruzzi Spur" as the most feasible route, even climbing a little way up it, it was clear that K2 was too high and too difficult for climbers at that time. But experience in high-altitude mountaineering developed quickly during the 1920s. At the same time, many areas that had been blank on the Karakoram map were explored. Veteran mountaineer, Eric Shipton, with a small party, reached the northern foot of K2 in 1937 and explored new ground, coming to the conclusion that any route from that side was impractical. But by 1938 climbers were ready to attempt K2 once more. Three major attempts were made before anyone succeeded.

1938 attempt

Charles Houston's capable 1938 team was a reconnaissance for a 1939 attempt. Bill House led the climb up a difficult rock chimney that would later be named for him. They pitched their highest camp, Camp 7, just below the Shoulder. Houston and one other team member probed a little higher before turning back exhausted.

A DIFFICULT CLIMB
House's Chimney is the technical crux of the route. A wide chimney in a steep wall narrows to a difficult ice-choked crack with little protection.

ATTEMPTS TO REACH THE SUMMIT			
YEAR	TEAM	ROUTE	HEIGHT REACHED
1902	Oscar Eckenstein, Anglo-Austrian	N.E. Ridge	21,400 feet (6,500 m)
1909	Duke of Abruzzi, Italian	S.E. Ridge (Abruzzi Spur)	20,000 feet (6,000 m)
1938	Charles Houston, USA	Abruzzi Spur	25,600 feet (7,800 m)
1939	Fritz Wiessner, USA	Abruzzi Spur	27,500 feet (8,400 m)
1953	Charles Houston, USA	Abruzzi Spur	25,000 feet (7,600 m)

In Training
Pre-expedition training in the Alps: Erich Abram (left) with Lino Lacedelli, a guide and ski-instructor, and Achille Compagnoni, a guide and ex-Alpine trooper in the Italian Army.

Struggle to the Summit

While Compagnoni and Lacedelli set up Camp 9, Bonatti and a Hunza porter, Mahdi, were bringing up more oxygen from below to deliver to them. But Camp 9 was higher than planned, night fell before they could reach it, and Bonatti and Mahdi endured a grim bivouac in the open at 26,250 feet (8,000 m). In the morning they retreated; Mahdi was severely frost-bitten. Compagnoni and Lacedelli climbed down to collect the dumped oxygen cylinders, ascended the rock beside the Bottleneck, crossed the Traverse, and eventually reached the summit.

Views From the Climb
Early morning at modern Camp 1 (below) on the Abruzzi Spur, the Godwin Austen Glacier already far below. On the summit (bottom) looking northeast toward the Aghil Range and China.

Dangerous Mountain

D anger is ever-present on a big mountain, affecting even expert climbers. Falls due to carelessness are rare; the main dangers come from nature. Storms can be killers, particularly on K2 where the high camps are easily cut off. Both mind and body deteriorate swiftly at high altitude where pulmonary edema, a life-threatening condition, phlebitis, and some other potentially fatal ailments are impossible to treat. Avalanche danger is always present and while unstable new snow is dangerous, Karakoram ice avalanches can be unpredictable and horrific. All ice gradually moves downhill and when a serac finally collapses it sweeps all before it. Concealed snow bridges, which are almost impossible to detect, can collapse, sending climbers falling into a deep crevasse.

WOMEN AT THE SUMMIT OF K2

1986	Wanda Rutkiewicz, Poland	Died later on Kangchenjunga
1986	Liliane Barrard, France	Killed while descending
1986	Julie Tullis, England	Died in storm on descent
1992	Chantel Maudit, France	Died later on Dhaulagiri
1992	Alison Hargreaves, England	Died in storm on descent
2004	Edurne Pasaban, Spain	
2006	Nives Meroi, Italy	
2006	Yuka Komatsu, Japan	
2007	Eun-Sun Oh, Korea	
2008	Cecilie Skog, Norway	
2008	Mi-Sun Go, Korea	Died later on Nanga Parrbat

At first it was said that there was a jinx on the women who had climbed K2, but high altitude mountaineering is always a dangerous activity. Up to and including the 2008 season a total of 302 people had reached the summit of K2, 31 of whom had been killed descending.

DEVASTATING FORCE

This avalanche (left), born of a small serac collapse high on K2, has swept down more than 6,500 feet (2,000 m) to become a lethal mass of powdered ice traveling at astonishing speed.

CREVASSE RESCUE

Once a rope can be got down to a fallen climber he should be able to climb to the surface, assuming no serious injury. This strenuous technique requires a jumar device or prusik knot, which slides up a rope but locks under tension.

Serious Challenge

Many consider K2 the most beautiful, probably the most difficult, and undoubtedly the most dangerous of the world's fourteen highest peaks—those above 26,000 feet (8,000 m). A climber has to be not only competent but also well acclimatized to get high enough on K2 to make a summit bid. But 23,000 feet (7,000 m) is no place to wait for better weather, and a storm at 26,000 feet (8,000 m) is a fight for survival. Descending is particularly dangerous. Once the summit has been reached adrenalin is exhausted, tiredness dulls the senses, and gathering dusk makes finding the route more difficult.

COURAGEOUS AND SKILLED

Wanda Rutkiewicz, from Poland, was the leading female climber of her generation. She reached the summit of K2 in 1986, descending safely when 13 others died. She disappeared attempting Kangchenjunga, solo, in 1992.

K2'S DEADLY TOLL

Alison Hargreaves, an English mother of two with a fine alpine record, climbed Everest solo, without oxygen, in 1995. But three months later she was blown to her death descending from the summit of K2 in a violent storm.

Everest

Roof of the World

The highest mountain in the world, rising to a peak of 29,035 feet (8,850 m), around 6 miles (10 km) above sea level, Mount Everest rises out of the Himalayan mountain range, bordering China and Nepal. It was formed around 60 million years ago, when undersea movement pushed the ocean's crust up and out of the sea. Climbers continue to be fascinated by Everest and to use their strength and skill to scale its terrifying heights. Everest is 784 feet (239 m) higher than K2, the world's second-highest mountain.

HIMALAYA FACT FILE	
Area	320,000 square miles (612,020 km2)
Length	1,500 miles (2,400 km)
Country borders crossed	India, Pakistan, China, Bhutan, Nepal
Major rivers that rise here	Indus, Ganges, Tsangpo/Brahmaputra, Rong, Yamuna, Chenab, Sutlej
No. of world's highest peaks	10 of the world's 14 highest

How Everest formed

The Himalayas are the youngest and highest mountain range on the planet. The theory of plate tectonics explains how the range was created from the collision of India (Indian Plate) and Asia (Asiatic Plate). These plates, which slide around on the fluid-like asthenosphere, are still moving approximately 3–5 inches (50–100 mm) each year.

WHEN PLATES COLLIDE

India starts its journey
India broke away from the great southern continent, Gondwana, about 145 million years ago and began its northward journey towards Eurasia.

Ocean-to-continent subduction
As India approached Eurasia, its seafloor subducted beneath the continental land-mass. A line of volcanoes developed along the edge of the Eurasian plate.

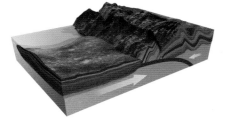

Collision begins
India was pushed against Eurasia. Seafloor sediments trapped between the continents were compressed and pushed upward, marking the birth of the Himalayas.

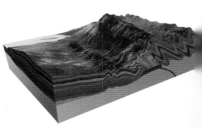

Folding and uplift
Compression continued, turning the sediment into metamorphic rock, squeezing it upward and outward along thrust faults over the adjacent continents. This continues today.

What is Everest made of?

Unbelievably, the summit of Mount Everest is actually made up of marine limestone, part of an ancient seabed that now sits on top of huge metamorphic rocks. The top of the world's highest mountain is, in fact, covered with clam, ammonite and trilobite fossils. When climbers plant their flags on the snowy summit, that snow lies over rock containing the skeletal remains of creatures that fell to the seabed, fossilized 200 million years ago and were then thrust upwards by the collision of continental plates. Sir Edmund Hillary verified that the rocks within the top 3,000 feet (1,000 m) of Mount Everest contain fossilized sea shells.

FOSSIL PROOF
Until recently, the theory of plate tectonics was just that—a theory. No-one could prove it until explorers such as those who attempted Mount Everest were able to bring back rock samples from the summit for geologists to study. Their theory was borne out by the fossil evidence.

PEAKS AND RIVERS

EVEREST
Close to the summit of Mount Everest the rock is made of marine limestone. Some fossil seams are up to 10 feet (3 m) deep.

RONGBUK GLACIER
The Rongbuk Glacier system is the main highway to the northern foot of the mountain. Climbers follow the tributary East Rongbuk Glacier on their way to the North Col and the North Ridge.

NUPTSE
Also known as West Peak, Nuptse's crest forms the southern wall of the Western Cwm, opposite the great flank of Everest. Camps 1 and 2 are dwarfed by its fearsome precipices.

RONG RIVER
The Rong drains the entire Rongbuk Glacier system northward. But instead of joining the mighty Tsangpo river, which flows parallel with the Himalaya to the north, it flows into the Arun, one of several rivers which, having cut gorges through the Himalayan range, flows eventually to the Ganges.

Conquering
Everest
...FAMOUS ATTEMPTS

George Leigh Mallory

Andrew Irvine

George Mallory was a talented and experienced climber when he attempted to climb Mount Everest in June 1924. He was regarded as particularly skillful and he was also very determined. His climbing partner, Andrew Irvine, was much younger and a less experienced mountaineer but he was an outstanding athlete. Irvine also brought excellent technical skills to the team—he was able to keep their oxygen cylinders in good working order although he did not have any access to spare parts. But despite years of planning and their high standard of physical fitness Mallory and Irvine died very high on the mountain.

Timeline of attempts in the 1920s

1921
A team of British climbers conducted a reconnaissance of Everest's north face and saw the sweeping East Rongbuk Glacier. They climbed by this route and reached the North Col.

1922
The British again made an attempt on Everest. Mallory led one team without extra oxygen and reached 26,900 feet (8,200 m). A second team, on a slightly different line, reached 27,300 feet (8,320 m) using extra oxygen.

1924
At the third British attempt George Mallory and Andrew Irvine climbed higher than all previous British attempts, but they disappeared. Two other team members, Howard Somervell and Edward Norton also made an attempt. Norton, alone, reached 28,100 feet (8,570 m), without extra oxygen, before turning back.

Acclimatization

One of the keys to climbing, and surviving, at high altitudes is to allow the body to become acclimatized to thin air. For this reason many climbers spend a couple of weeks at higher-than-usual altitudes before tackling a high-altitude climb. Gradually their blood adapts to the conditions and is able to carry more oxygen than usual in each red blood cell. Practice climbs are helpful in other ways as well; a climber can carry equipment up to a high camp for use during the final ascent. Reinhold Messner spent seven weeks at an altitude of more than 16,500 feet (5,000 m) becoming acclimatized to the thin air before his solo ascent in 1980. Two years earlier he had made the first oxygen-free ascent, with climbing partner, Peter Habeler.

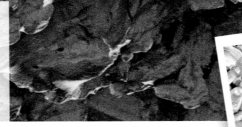

FROSTBITE HAZARD

Messner checks his frostbitten thumb. When skin is exposed to temperatures below 32°F (0°C) there is danger of frostbite. The fingers, toes, nose, and ears are particularly susceptible.

KHUMBU ICEFALL

The tiny figures of Messner and Habeler in the Khumbu Icefall show how challenging this part of the Everest climb is. The Khumbu Glacier, which forms the icefall, moves at such speed that crevasses open with little warning.

MESSNER'S ASCENTS OF THE WORLD'S HIGHEST PEAKS

YEAR	PEAK	HEIGHT
1970	Nanga Parbat, Pakistan	26,657 feet (8,125 m)
1972	Manaslu, Nepal	26,781 feet (8,163 m)
1975	Gasherbrum, Pakistan/China	26,470 feet (8,068 m)
1977	Dhaulagiri,* Nepal	26,795 feet (8,167 m)
1978	Mount Everest, Nepal/China	29,035 feet (8,850 m)
1979	K2, Pakistan/China	28,251 feet (8,611 m)
1980	Mount Everest,** Nepal/China	29,035 feet (8,850 m)
1981	Shisha Pangma, China	26,397 feet (8,046 m)
1982	Kanchenjunga, Nepal/India	28,168 feet (8,586 m)
1982	Gasherbrum II, Pakistan/China	26,362 feet (8,035 m)
1982	Broad Peak, Pakistan/China	26,401 feet (8,047 m)
1983	Cho Oyu, Nepal/China	26,905 feet (8,201 m)
1985	Annapurna, Nepal	26,544 feet (8,091 m)
1985	Dhaulagiri, Nepal	26,795 feet (8,167 m)
1986	Makalu, Nepal/China	27,766 feet (8,463 m)
1986	Lhotse, Nepal/China	27,940 feet (8,516 m)

All without extra oxygen.   *Summit not reached   ** Solo

HILLARY'S TEAM

The teamwork between Tenzing and Hillary was essential to their successful climb; both were true team players. But it was the teamwork shown by the entire expedition that really made the successful climb possible.

into the death zone

THE ROOF OF THE WORLD

At the summit of the highest mountain, Mount Everest, in the world's highest mountain range, the Himalaya, climbers stand on marine limestone—rock that was once on the seafloor. As the Eurasian and Indo-Australian plates collided some 60 million years ago, the seafloor was thrust upward. The pressure continues to push the mountains higher to this day.

> *" It was a prodigious white fang... From the jaw of the world, we saw Mount Everest."*
>
> GEORGE MALLORY

SOUTH COL ROUTE

"We stepped up. We were there. The dream had come true." TENZING NORGAY

Since the summit of Everest was first reached by Tenzing Norgay and Edmund Hillary in 1953, hundreds of climbers have followed this route to the top. Some say that the South Col Route is a little more dangerous than the North Ridge Route, mainly because the Khumbu Icefall is so unstable. The route through the icefall changes daily since it is constantly moving. In the dawn, the safest time, the cold in the icefall and the Western Cwm is intense, but by midday the sun reflecting from the snowy flanks of Everest,

Lhotse, and Nuptse can raise the air temperature to as much as 100°F (38°C).

The climb up the Lhotse Face requires a major effort and tired climbers clip onto fixed ropes to assist the ascent and safeguard against potentially fatal falls. Climbers usually start using oxygen above Camp 3 on the Lhotse Face, before the route bears upward and across to the South Col. Here, wide open to the elements, there are likely to be a couple of dozen tents from several expeditions pitched on a stony area about the size of a football field.

Camp 4 on the South Col

▲ EVEREST
▲ LHOTSE
▲ NUPTSE

Climate in the Himalaya

Hundreds of peaks rise more than 23,000 feet (7,000 m) in the Himalaya, many still unclimbed and even unnamed. Bringing the rains to the Indian subcontinent, the annual summer monsoon falls as heavy snow on the southern flanks of the higher mountains, while the northern flanks, in the rain shadow, are not much affected. Both summer and winter snows feed the thousands of glaciers that give birth to many of Asia's great rivers.

GUIDED EXPEDITIONS

With guided expeditions leading climbers to the summit via both the Nepalese South Col route and the Chinese North East Ridge, dozens of climbers may be on the mountain on the one day. This causes delays on the fixed ropes sections where progress must be one-at-a-time.

Mountain Weather

Everest rises into the Jet Stream, the narrow band of very high winds that frequently encircles the planet at that latitude above 26,000 feet (8,000 m), so any attempt on the summit is governed by both wind and weather. Apart from the usual winter snowfall, the Nepal Himalaya are also subject to the summer monsoon which brings a second season of heavy snowfall to the mountains from June until early September.

Originally it was thought that there was only one weather window for climbing, in the short period of calm before the onset of the monsoon in early June. But in the 1950s it was realised that there is another fairly stable period after the monsoon in late September. In fact post-monsoon weather is typically more stable, though far colder, than pre-monsoon weather. Modern clothing and equipment help climbers to withstand the cold and there are now two official weather windows on Everest, pre- and post-monsoon.

WEATHER CONDITIONS ON EVEREST	
Temperature	January. Summit temperature averages –33°F (–36°C); it can be as low as –76°F (–60°C).
	July. Summit temperature average –2°F (–19°C).
Wind speed	Oct.–Mar. Almost constant Category 1 Hurricane: 75 mph (150 km/h)
	Jun.–Sept. Almost no wind at all: 11mph (24 km/h)

J F M A M J J A S O N D

–32°F (–36°C)   –29°F (–34°C)

This mountain is best climbed in May and June or September

CLIMBING SEASONS

The extreme altitude means that the air temperature is much lower than most other places on Earth. Added to this, the high winds and the resulting wind-chill factor make conditions on Mount Everest demanding for all climbers.

What triggers an avalanche?

An avalanche can happen wherever snow is lying at a steep angle, on slopes of 30–45°, but large avalanches can also occur on slopes as gentle as 25°. Snow is unstable during and after snowfalls or after prolonged heating by the sun, especially on steep inclines; and snow falling at a rate of 1 inch (2 cm) or more per hour increases the risk of avalanche. Most frightening are ice avalanches, which are unpredictable. Himalayan ice cliffs are "rubbery", tending to lean a long way before they finally collapse, hurling down huge chunks of ice that sweep all before them.

MOUNT McKinley

The Great One

DRAMATIC SKYLINE
Having reached the summit of Mount McKinley, at 20,320 feet (6,194 m) the highest peak in North America, two climbers carefully descend the summit ridge toward Denali Pass.

MASSIVE MOUNTAIN
Mount McKinley, its South and North summits conspicuous, is seen here from a distance of some 50 miles (80 km). This view is from the northeast near Polychrome Mountain on the Denali Highway.

Named after the 25th President of the United States but known to the indigenous Alaskans as Denali ("The Great One"), Mount McKinley is a colossal, icy complex of ridges, spurs, buttresses, and hanging glaciers. It rises to twin summits, dwarfing the other peaks of the Alaska Range. Situated between the warm, damp Pacific and the cold Alaskan interior, the mountain, just 150 miles (240 km) from the Arctic Circle, is a crucible of particularly evil weather. Several early attempts to climb Mount McKinley failed. One group of climbers, in 1906, claimed to have reached the summit but this was later found to have been a deception. In 1910 a party of six did reach the North Summit but it was not until 1913 that Hudson Stuck, Archdeacon of the Yukon, with three companions, claimed the South Summit 850 feet (259 m) higher. The few climbers who reached the summit before 1951 followed a route on the mountain's northeast side, via the Muldrow Glacier.

APPROACHING THE SUMMIT

At just above 16,000 feet (4,800 m), a climber slowly ascends the West Buttress crest, the Regular Route used by most parties. The previous camp can be seen in the Genet Basin far below. Mount Foraker, the second highest peak in the Alaska Range, rises beyond.

CREVASSE DANGER

Even on flat glaciers the crevasses are deep and often hidden. Wise climbers travel roped-up so that if they do fall into a crevasse they have a good chance of climbing back to the top.

GLACIER HIGHWAY

Except in emergency, aircraft are forbidden to land on glaciers in the declared wilderness area surrounding Mount McKinley, so climbers face long ski approaches up highly crevassed glacier highways. Towing their equipment on pulques—simple lightweight sleds originating in Lappland—these climbers descend the Muldrow Glacier.

Locating Mount McKinley

The culminating peak of the 400-mile (644-km) Alaska Range, Mount McKinley stands at the heart of the Denali National Park. It is only 130 miles (210 km) from the state capital, Anchorage.

Highest Peak in North America

Its summit standing well above others in the surrounding range, the scale of Mount McKinley is truly Himalayan, and its location, close to the Arctic Circle, accentuates the effects of high altitude—ice, blizzards, thin air, avalanches. Dozens of challenging routes up the mountain attract the world's best mountaineers. Most celebrated is the Cassin Rib on the South Face, which was first climbed by an Italian team in 1961. They took 23 days to reach the summit, establishing a number of camps as they climbed. Strict Park Service regulations govern access and climbing within the National Park; climbing permits must be applied for in advance.

AIR TRANSPORT

Most climbing parties charter ski-equipped light planes to fly them onto flat glaciers below the mountain where landing is permitted. They usually depart from Talkeetna, a rail- and road-head some 60 miles (97 km) away.

SOUTH PEAK
20,320ft (6,194

SOUTH FACE

HARPER GLACIER

KARSTENS RIDGE

HARPEN ICEFALL

EAST BUTTRESS

MOUNT CARPÉ

MOUNT TATUM

TRALEIKA GLACIER

MOUNTAIN BIRDLIFE

The ground-nesting ptarmigan (*Lagopus lagopus*) is the official Alaska state bird. Its mottled plumage provides good camouflage in summer; in winter it turns white to avoid detection on the snow.

MULDROW GLACIER

McGONAGALL PASS

Dall sheep (*Ovis dalli*)

48

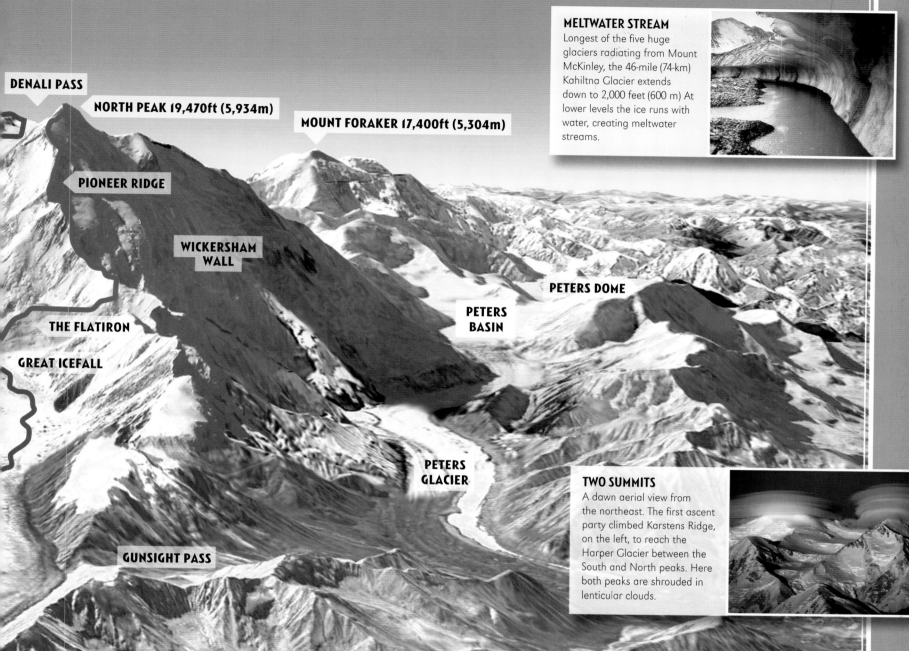

DENALI PASS

NORTH PEAK 19,470ft (5,934m)

MOUNT FORAKER 17,400ft (5,304m)

PIONEER RIDGE

WICKERSHAM WALL

PETERS DOME

PETERS BASIN

THE FLATIRON

GREAT ICEFALL

PETERS GLACIER

GUNSIGHT PASS

The Climb to the Summit

A strenuous effort is needed to reach Mount McKinley's summit, yet hundreds of people climb the West Buttress Route every year, many of them in guided parties. Entirely on snow, the non-technical climb usually requires five camps. But the climb to the summit and back to base camp is not without danger, particularly from bad weather. The schedule for a typical guided party is 20 days. Experienced, acclimatized mountaineers could complete the climb in 10 days. The adjacent West Rib, more direct and technical, is popular with competent climbers. The South Face routes and the longer ridges are serious and committing expeditions.

Grizzly bear (Ursus horribilis)

Matterhorn

A Rocky Peak

The Matterhorn, or Monte Cervino in Italian, is the epitome of mountain form, carved over the eons by fierce glacial erosion from all sides. Mountains of similar shape, formed in the same way, are known as Matterhorn Peaks. The Matterhorn's name and distinctive shape are familiar everywhere. At 14,690 feet (4,478 m) it is only the fourteenth highest mountain in the European Alps but, as it stands aloof and almost completely isolated, it captures the imagination of all who see it; it has long been a popular subject for photographers. Long narrow valleys approach the mountain's foot from the north and south, cradling at their heads the villages of Zermatt and Breuil (Cervinia), both prime ski resorts. Since Roman times the two valleys have been connected by the Theodule Pass, 10,825 feet (3,300 m). It is a straightforward summer hike for those accustomed to glacier crossing and, with the proximity of ski lifts in winter, it is a route frequently used by recreational skiers visiting the neighboring resort over the frontier.

Edward Whymper

Edward Whymper first visited Zermatt in 1860 and became keenly interested in mountaineering. At that time no one had climbed to the Matterhorn's summit and Whymper made that one of his goals. He also made many other notable first ascents throughout the Western Alps. After 1865 he went exploring and climbing elsewhere, making first ascents in Greenland, the Canadian Rockies, and the Andes. He died in 1911.

WHYMPER'S ATTEMPTS ON THE MATTERHORN		
Date	Height reached	Route
Aug 29–30, 1861	12,650 feet (3,856 m)	Italian Ridge
July 7–8, 1862	12,000 feet (3,658 m)	Italian Ridge
July 9–10, 1862	12,992 feet (3,960 m)	Italian Ridge
July 18–19, 1862	13,400 feet (4,084 m)	Italian Ridge
July 23–24, 1862	13,150 feet (4,008 m)	Italian Ridge
July 25–26, 1862	13,460 feet (4,103 m)	Italian Ridge
Aug 10–11, 1863	13,280 feet (4,048 m)	Italian Ridge
June 21, 1865	11,200 feet (3,414 m)	East Face

Heavy Weather

Mountain weather is always fickle. The Pennine Alps, a major European watershed dividing warm Italy and the Mediterranean from the tangled mountains and glaciers of Switzerland, are no exception. A clash of airstreams—warm or cold, humid or dry—occurs constantly. Astride that watershed, the isolated tooth of the Matterhorn attracts frequent thunderstorms that play around its summit while Zermatt, in the valley below, is bathed in sunshine. The lightning is dangerous and is often heralded by a strange humming sound that comes from ice axes and other metal equipment. If this happens it is a good idea to temporarily dump anything metallic and take shelter below a ridge or a projecting rock.

EXTRA DANGER
In a bad storm, even a straightforward climb can be a fight for survival. This picture (left) was taken during a storm on the Matterhorn's difficult North Face.

Whymper as Artist

A talented artist, Whymper was apprenticed to his father's wood engraving business in London when publications were still illustrated with engravings. A drawing commission for Longmans Publishers first brought him to the Alps. After 1865 he illustrated many books and wrote several of his own, notably *Scrambles Amongst the Alps*. It is considered to be among the finest mountaineering books ever written.

Whymper's engraving "The Matterhorn from the Riffelberg" (left). This, and the other illustrations (below) are from his book *Scrambles Amongst the Alps*.

Whymper illustrates a fall he took while descending from the Tete du Lion after his solo attempt of July 19, 1862. Luckily he was not badly injured.

Locating the Matterhorn
The Matterhorn is one of the knot of high, free-standing mountains at the eastern extremity of the Pennine Alps, the chain of mountains that forms part of the Swiss-Italian border.

[Map labels:]
Montreaux
Lake Geneva
Bernese Alps
Sierre
Valley
Visp
Rhone
Sion
Rhone
Rhone
SWITZERLAND
Saas Fee
Martigny
Weisshorn 14,782ft (4,505m)
Dom 14,913ft (4,545m)
Verbier
Arolla
Dent Blanche 14,295ft (4,357m)
Zermatt
Matterhorn 14,690ft (4,478m)
Grand Combin 14,154ft (4,314m)
Monte Rosa 15,203ft (4,634m)
RANCE
Great St. Bernard Pass
Breuil
Chamonix-Mont-Blanc
Mont Blanc 15,771ft (4,807m)
Pennine Alps
Aosta
ITALY

DAWN LIGHT

Its dramatic summit cone alight with the rays of a rising sun, the Matterhorn dominates its landscape. The mountain's steep rock ridges are an irresistible challenge for climbers.

The Summit

By 1865 the Matterhorn was the last of the great peaks that had still not been climbed. Most persistent of the English amateurs and local Italian guides, who for several years had been competing to make the first ascent, were Edward Whymper the Englishman and Jean-Antoine Carrel from Breuil. Eleven attempts were made on the Italian Ridge, which appeared to be the easiest route, before the summit was finally reached via the Hornli Ridge. Whymper teamed up with Rev. Charles Hudson, Douglas Hadow, Lord Francis Douglas, and their respective guides and led them to the summit on July 14, 1865. A terrible accident on the descent became the most analyzed and controversial in mountaineering history. Accusations were made that a vital rope had been cut, but in fact it was a worn-out spare used by mistake.

SHAPE OF THE MOUNTAIN

The mountain has four well-defined ridges and four steep faces. The Swiss summit stands at the eastern end of the 260-foot (80-m) summit crest, the Italian, a few feet (one metre) lower, at its western end.

VIEW FROM THE SOUTHEAST
An engraving of Whymper's showing the Matterhorn from the Theodule Pass. The mountain rises steeply on each side.

AT THE TOP
Gustave Doré's drawing of the successful arrival at the summit. The chief competitors in the race to the top were still far below.

Hudson
Rev. Charles Hudson was one of the greatest pioneer climbers.

Hadow
Hudson's 19-year-old protégé, Douglas Hadow, was a novice climber.

Croz
Michel Croz, the finest Chamonix guide of the age.

Douglas
Lord Francis Douglas, an experienced climber, was the second son of Lord Queensbury.

Fatal Descent

The fatal accident occurred on the exposed ground above the Shoulder, a succession of small ledges separated by short steps and dusted with snow. Descending carefully, Croz led with Hadow next, then Hudson and Douglas. The two other guides, both named Taugwalder, and Whymper followed. All were roped together but modern belays were unknown. It seems that Croz was assisting Hadow when the latter slipped, knocking Croz from his footing. The tight rope jerked Hudson and then Douglas from their holds. Whymper and the Taugwalders braced themselves to hold the fall but the rope snapped behind Douglas. The four men plunged down the North Face.

Many Routes to the Top

The ascent of the Matterhorn, last of the great peaks to be climbed, ended the "Golden Age of Alpinism" (1854–1865) and climbers started to explore other, more difficult, routes to the summit. This so-called "Silver Age" continued into the 1900s. Almost invariably the early mountaineers had climbed with guides, originally local peasants who understood the terrain. The best of these soon became a corps of elite, skilled mountaineers who developed a proud tradition of comradeship and teamwork with their employers. But this relationship was already disappearing by the beginning of the 20th century as guideless climbing became the norm and guides became paid leaders rather than respected partners. Today hundreds of fit but inexperienced climbers are guided up the Matterhorn's many routes every season.

ALPINE GUIDES
Most alpine centers have their own licenced and qualified guides; in alpine countries many of the best amateurs take the international guides exams. There are also fully qualified and often expert alpine guides from elsewhere, particularly Britain. Today most guides supplement their income by working as ski instructors or ski-tour leaders in winter.

Whymper and Carrel
Edward Whymper's guide, Jean-Antoine Carrel, lowers him over an overhang. Guides need to be both strong and skillful.

SCHMID BROTHERS

In 1931, on their first visit to the Western Alps, Franz and Toni Schmid, brothers from Munich, climbed the intimidating Matterhorn North Face with only one bivouac. The climb was repeated only twice in 15 years.

The Alpine Club

The original Alpine Club was founded in 1857 with premises in London. Club members must be experienced mountaineers and the membership includes leading climbers from many nations. National alpine clubs were also founded in the 19th century—Austrian in 1862, Swiss and Italian in 1863, French in 1874. These clubs own most of the alpine huts and members enjoy reciprocal rights.

Gear and techniques

Primitive at first, climbing equipment, clothing, and techniques improved only gradually. Hemp ropes were useful for safety but they did not guarantee survival in a fall. On steep ice, steps had to be cut. Major developments occurred in the Eastern Alps in the early 1900s, where difficult rock climbs produced innovative rope techniques and inspired new gear such as pitons and carabiners. These were soon used on the big mountains too. Nylon ropes, first seen in the late 1940s, revolutionized climbing. Modern ice tools originated in Scotland in the 1960s and 1970s.

Modern crampons are twelve-pointed and tungsten-tipped, with quick-release bindings.

Modern ice screws (ice pitons) are tubular and threaded.

Whymper's own crampons and heavy, wood-shafted, ice axes c 1865

Specialist ice tools—hammer and adze, designed for climbing vertical frozen waterfalls

Modern ropes, man-made fiber, sheathed "kernmantle" construction

Carabiners—lightweight snap links of high-tech alloy with twist-lock gates.

High-altitude climbs are serious undertakings. Careful planning, technical skill, and good weather conditions are just some of the factors that must be taken into account. But the pioneers, those who reached the summit of a challenging mountain for the first time, also had great courage. They were pathfinders in unknown terrain.

Alpine Climbing Grades

The difficulty of Alpine climbs is usually described by the French *Vallot* system. This is adjectival and takes into account the seriousness, length, dangers and commitment necessary, as well as the difficulty. A numerical grade from l to Vl, with + or – as appropriate, is added to cover the technical difficulties of the hardest individual rock pitches in normal conditions. Ice routes, on which conditions can vary from hour to hour, are covered only by the adjectival grade

Facile **F** easy snow plods and very easy scrambles–rope not usually necessary except on crevassed glaciers.

Peu Difficile **PD** steeper snow climbs and straightforward rock climbs where the rope would normally be used.

example: Eiger, West flank Regular route= PD
Matterhorn, Hornli Ridge = PD, pitches of II

Assez Difficile **AD** routes with a number of difficulties requiring some experience.
example: Eiger, Mittellegi Ridge = AD, pitches of III
Matterhorn, Italian Ridge = AD, pitches of II
Matterhorn, Zmutt Ridge = AD+, pitches of II

Difficile **D** more serious climbs on snow and ice with definite technical problems.
example: Eiger, Mittellegi Ridge without the fixed ropes = D, pitches of IV

Tres Difficile **TD** serious climbs with sustained technical difficulties demanding commitment and considerable experience.
example: Eiger, Lauper Route = TD, pitches of III

Extremement Difficile **ED** the most serious, sustained, and committing climbs of the highest technical difficulties, likely to be long and encountering objective dangers.
example: Eiger. Nordwand 1938 route = ED, pitches of V
Matterhorn North Face = ED -, pitches of IV–V

SOME OF THE GREAT ALPINE PEAKS Date of first ascent

DATE	PEAK	HEIGHT	COMMENTS
1786	Mont Blanc	15,771 ft (4,807 m)	highest mountain in the Alps
1811	Jungfrau	13,642 ft (4,158 m)	–
1812	Finsteraarhorn	14,022 ft (4,274 m)	highest mountain in the Bernese Alps
1855	Monte Rosa	15,203 ft (4,634 m)	highest peak in Switzerland - 2nd in the Alps by Rev.Charles Hudson et al
1855	Mont Blanc du Tacul	13,937 ft (4,248 m)	by Rev. Charles Hudson et al
1858	Dom	14,912 ft (4,454 m)	highest mountain entirely in Switzerland
1859	Grand Combin	14,153 ft (4,314 m)	–
1859	Aletschhorn	13,763 ft (4,195 m)	–
1860	Gran Paradiso	13,323 ft (4,061 m)	highest mountain entirely in Italy
1861	Weisshorn	14,782 ft (4,506 m)	–
1861	Liskamm	14,852 ft (4,527 m)	–
1861	Schreckhorn	13,379 ft (4,078 m)	–
1862	Dent Blanche	14,293 ft (4,357 m)	–
1863	Dent d'Herens	13,685 ft (4,171 m)	–
1864	Zinal Rothorn	13,849 ft (4,221 m)	–
1865	Aiguille Verte	13,523 ft (4,122 m)	by Edward Whymper + party
1865	Obergabelhorn	13,330 ft (4,063 m)	2nd ascent one day after the 1st, by Lord Francis Douglas
1865	Grandes Jorasses	13,727 ft (4,184 m)	by Edward Whymper + party
1865	Matterhorn	14,690 ft (4,478 m)	by Edward Whymper + party

EVEREST MILESTONES

SUCCESSFUL EXPEDITION	YEAR	EXPEDITION NATIONALITY	ROUTE	CLIMBERS	COMMENTS
1	1953	British	Western Cwm—South Col —S.E.Ridge	Edmund Hillary (NZ) Tenzing Norgay (Sherpa)	First ascent of Everest by the now standard route from Nepal
2	1956	Swiss	Western Cwm—South Col —S.E.Ridge	Adolf Reist, Hans von Gunten	Second ascent of Everest—two pairs to the summit on successive days
3	1960	Chinese	North Col	Wang Fu-chou, Gonpa, Chu Yin-hua	First ascent from the North using the route attempted by seven British expeditions in the 1920s and 1930s. Now the standard northern route
4	1963	American	West Ridge (Hornbein Couloir on North Face reached from the Western Cwm via the West Ridge).	Tom Hornbein, Willy Unsoeld	First ascent of a new route, descending by South Col. A bold first traverse of the mountain
8	1975	Japanese	Western Cwm—South Col —S.E.Ridge	Junko Tabei (with Ang Tshering Sherpa)	First female ascent
10	1975	British	Southwest Face	Dougal Haston Doug Scott	First ascent of both a new route and a major Himalayan Face
28	1979	Slovenian	West Ridge Integrale—the Direct Route following the West Ridge all the way.	Nejc Zaplotnik Andrej Stremfelj	First ascent of a major ridge involving difficult technical rock climbing.
33	1983	American	Kangshung or East Face	Kim Momb, Lou Reichardt, Carlos Buhler	First ascent of both a new route and a major Himalayan Face
37	1984	Australian	North Face via the Great Couloir (also known as 'Norton's Couloir')	Tim Macartney-Snape Greg Mortimer	First ascent of a new route taking a direct line up the North Face. Climbed without supplementary oxygen.

Expedition Tactics

There are basically three methods for attempting to climb a very large mountain.

Siege Tactics involve placing a chain of camps up the mountain, each supporting the next. The traditional method still used by large expeditions.

Using **Capsule Tactics** a single, self-contained, self-supporting camp is moved higher and higher up the mountain. A bold and environmentally friendly technique for a small team

Alpine Style, the method used in the Alps and now even on Everest. One, two, or possibly more climbers "go for it", moving fast and light, bivouacking where necessary and snatching the summit. Very bold, very ethical —the modern style.

Glossary

Abseil
Literally "down-rope" in German, a rapid method of descent using the rope to slide down but controlling the slide by friction.

Altitude sickness
Illness suffered at altitudes where the air is thin. It can range from headaches, at lower altitudes, to potentially fatal conditions.

Belay
The dynamic rope-handling technique used by a climber to safeguard himself and his companions from a fall. Also the rock spike or piton used to attach the rope.

Bivouac
A temporary overnight camp in the open.

Carabiner
An oval or D-shaped snap-link usually made from lightweight alloy, which opens with a sprung gate.

Chimney
A vertical fissure, usually in rock and at least wide enough to admit the body.

Chock
A small metal wedge that is placed in a crack as a means of attachment to rock. Easily removed without damaging the rock.

Couloir
A gully on a mountainside, usually snow- or ice filled. May be a steep chute and therefore a natural channel for falling rocks and avalanche.

Crevasse
A crack, which may be deep, in the surface of a glacier or icefield. When bridged with snow a crevasse is difficult to detect.

Cwm
The universally adopted Welsh name for a deep valley head, a hanging valley of glacial origin. Also "cirque".

Hanging icefield
A miniature glacier apparently stuck onto the face of a mountain, likely to be less steep than the surrounding cliffs and walls.

Icefall
A cataract of ice, always moving, formed when a glacier flows over a rock step or steep ground or is constricted between mountain walls.

Jumar
A small metal device which, when clipped to a rope, will slide up it but not down.

Lenticular cloud
A lens- or wave-shaped cloud formed when warm air condenses as it rises over a mountain top.

Moraine
Rock debris, rubble and boulders brought down by a glacier, which may form long ridges or high mounds lying on, beside, or below the glacier. Often unstable.

Piton
A small metal spike, variously shaped, that can be hammered into a crack in the rock. Ice pitons, longer and tubular, are screwed into ice.

Prusik knot
A simple friction hitch. It can be freely pushed up when slack but locks under tension. Used for climbing a hanging rope.

Pulmonary edema
An excessive accumulation of fluid in the lungs caused by altitude. Fatal at high altitude, treatable by immediate descent.

Ski mountaineer
A mountaineer who climbs mountains on specially fitted skis. Even steep snow slopes can be ascended swiftly and easily.

Talus
Also known as scree. Loose rock fragments ranging in size from pebbles to small boulders. Usually found on the slopes below cliffs or on ledges.

Traverse
Moving sideways as opposed to upward or downward.

Watershed
The dividing line, usually following a ridge or high ground, between the catchments of two river systems.

Wind-chill
The cooling effect of wind causing an apparent temperature drop on exposed skin.

index

ABOUT THE AUTHOR

John Cleare

Addicted to mountaineering since schooldays, John Cleare
has climbed, skied and explored among the mountains of six
continents, led numerous expeditions and made first ascents in
the Alps, Africa, and the Himalaya. He has been a professional
photographer for 50 years and has an international reputation as
a mountain and wilderness photographer. He has made films
on the Matterhorn, the Eiger, Everest, and elsewhere, and his
picture archive, Mountain Camera, is well known.
John and his wife live in rural Wiltshire.

ACKNOWLEDGMENTS

Key t=top; l=left; r=right; tl=top left; tcl=top center left; tc=top
center; tcr=top center right; tr=top right; cl=center left; c=center;
cr=center right; b=bottom; bl=bottom left; bcl=bottom center left;
bc=bottom center; bcr=bottom center right; br=bottom right

Photos

ACPL = Alpine Club; ALA = Alamy; ASD = Audrey Salkeld; ASV
= As Verlag; CBT = Corbis; GI = Getty; HH = Hedgehog House;
IS = iStock Photo; JC = John Cleare; Jung = Jungfraujoch Railway;
KG = Kenny Grant; LD = Leo Dickinson; PUB = Public Domain;
RB = Robert Bosch; RDA = Rue Des Archive; REM = Reinhold
Messner; RGS = Royal Geographical Society; SDASM = San Diego
Air and Space Museum; SH = Shutterstock; TF = Top Foto; TPL =
The Photo Library

Cover SDASM;

1c RGS; 2bl iS; tr JC; 3c RB ; 4bc, cl GI; bl HH; tr iS; 5cr CBT; tl
GI; c HH; cl JC; 6t GI; 7bc CBT; bc, tl, tr JC; 8bc, cl JC; 9c GI;
tr iS; cr, tl, tr JC; bc TPL; 10c JC; 11tl ASD; tr ASV; bc, bl, br, br
JUNG; 12tc JC; cr PUB; 13bc, c, tl ASD; br, c JC; tr TPL; 14l RB;
b, b, bl JC; br LD; 15bl, c, cr JC; br TPL; 16tc JC; cr TF; 17tr JC;
bc, br, tl TF; 18cr, tc JC; 19br CBT; tl HH; tr JC; br SH; bc TPL;
20br, tc JC; cr TF; 21tl ASD; bc JC; 22tl CBT; 23tr CBT; tc SH;
24cl CBT; cl HH; bl SH; bl TPL; 25c CBT; 26tl JC; cr TF; 27br,
br JC; tr RDA; c TF; 28tc HH; 29tl CBT; c, tr, tr JC; br TF; 30c
GI; 31bc, bl, tc GI; bl JC; bc, cr TPL; 32tc GI; cr, cr KG; 33bc, br,
br, c, cr, cr, tl GI; 34br, cl, cr RGS; tl KG; 35bc, bc, cr, tl RGS; 36c,
cr TPL; 37tr RGS; tr TPL; 38cr ALA; br PUB; tc REM; 39bc ALA;
c GI; 40cl, cl, cl JC; 41cr CBT; c GI; cr JC; c, cr TPL; 42bc SH;
43br CBT; bc, bc GI; cl TPL; 44bc, bl, tr GI; 45c CBT; tl KH; tr
TPL; 46b, tc HH; 47cl CBT; c HH; tr JC; 48tr HH; bl, br SH;
49cr, tr CBT; br iS; bc TF; 50cr ACPL; tc TF; 51bc, br, cr, cr, cr, tl
JC; 52tc GI; 53tr ACPL; tl JC; bc, bl, c, c, cr TF; 54tc, tc RGS; cr
CBT; br, br JC; 55c ACPL; br, cr CBT; bl GI; tl, tr JC; 56tr CBT;
bc JC; 57br iS; tr TF; br TPL; 58tc CBT; br JC; 59br, c, cr, tl, tr
JC; 61b, HH.

Illustrations

Peter Bull Art Studio 6cr, 11tl, 11tc, 11br, 21c, 21br, 21tr, 25br,
52br, Digital elevation models: Christian Fremd, Geographx 8c, 9c,
22c, 23c, 24c, 25c, 36b, 37b, 40c, 41c, 42tr, 43c, 48c, 49c, 56c,
57c.